Vignettes

JAMES MONTGOMERY FLAGG

UNCLE SAM AND BEYOND

Nicholas Steward

Collectors Press, Inc.
Portland, Oregon

Acknowledgements

World War I poster reproductions from:
Poster Collection, Prints and Photographs Division,
Library of Congress. Special thanks to
Scott Campbell Steward and Faith Flagg.

Editor:
Michael Goldberg & Gail Manchur

Design:
Hoover H.Y. Li

Published by: Collectors Press, Inc.
P.O. Box 230986, Portland, OR 97281

Printed in Singapore

First American Edition

10 9 8 7 6 5 4 3 2 1

ISBN: 1-888054-07-7

James Montgomery Flagg

Born in the closing years of the last century, James Montgomery Flagg's slightly profane but self-confident nature mirrored this brash young country. America's unshakable creed at this time was "progress" and as a young man, Flagg eagerly embraced the newly-invented automobile and motion pictures. In his illustrations, he chronicled the changing mores of a post-Victorian society, especially the tension between the sexes as women's roles changed. But when the United States went to war in 1917 and then in 1941, he turned his brush away from the social and the comic to inspire, through his posters, Americans in their fight against tyranny.

The Bookman
April 1898

When he retired after World War II, Flagg was still a popular illustrator, having had a career that spanned over fifty years. This was a very long time in an industry where many careers were cut short by the public's ever-changing tastes. If his artistic successes alone are considered, Flagg is in the top rank of American illustrators, but his colorful personality and wit also make him one of the most interesting. Today

The Bookman
OUT
NOW
READ
THE
BOOKMAN
A Literary
:: Journal ::
PUBLISHED
MONTHLY
APRIL

Judge's Library
April 1898

Flagg is best known for his Uncle Sam *I Want You* poster. This striking image appears on everything from T-shirts to coffee mugs, but still remains a powerful symbol. As is revealed in the thirty images of Flagg's work in this Vignette, he was able to do much more--in fact, he produced over forty posters during World War I, and many more during World War II, along with hundreds of magazine covers, book illustrations, and

Life
April 16, 1908

advertisements. For many years Flagg produced, on average, a piece of artwork each day in pen and ink, watercolor or oils, while in the evenings he wrote articles, plays, and an occasional movie script.

This multi-faceted man was born on June 18, 1877, in Pelham Manor, New York. The Flaggs were of stout Puritan stock dating back to the seventeenth century, with some Scotch-Irish

Life
JAMES MONTGOMERY FLAGG

ancestry added to the mixture. There was little in his background to suggest a brash or artistic strain, but his precocity in art first manifested itself when he was two. At about the time he discovered his second love, the opposite sex, six years later, the young Flagg began painting landscapes around his family's summer house in Rutland, Massachusetts.

In the 1880s, his family moved a number of times between Brooklyn and

JAMES MONTGOMERY FLAGG

Life (Teddy Roosevelt)
June 16, 1910

Manhattan, with Flagg attending Dr. Chapin's school and then the Horace Mann school. While many of his contemporaries spent years struggling for recognition, success was not long in coming in his chosen field of illustration. At the age of eleven, in 1889, Flagg sold his first drawing to *St. Nicholas* magazine. The assistant editor had earlier seen something in the rough but lively portfolio Flagg had brought him and had encouraged his work. The first illustration that *St. Nicholas*

LIFE

PRICE 10 CENTS
VOL. LV, NO. 1442. JUNE 16, 191

bought, paying the happy youngster ten dollars, was a sketch of Latin axioms. Within a few years, Flagg was drawing humorous sketches for the weeklies *Judge* and *Life*.

"Monty was a nice boy 'til he went to the Art Students' League," his mother used to say. To which Flagg always responded that he was never "nice." At sixteen, he applied to the National Academy School but was rejected. He

Judge, **Oh Mother!**
May 20, 1911

then enrolled at the Art Students' League where he became great friends with two future illustrators, John Wolcott Adams and Walter Appleton Clark.

In later years he believed that all an artist needed, besides practice, was high school, art school, and some constructive "loafing" to observe the world rather than the more formal environment of art college. In a letter to the editor of The New York *Times* (September 8, 1929),

JUDGE

PRICE, 10 CENTS
MAY 20 1911

Judge Tickets?
June 10, 1911

Flagg recalled:

> I loafed 4 years at the Art Students' League, went to England, studied there and then a year in Paris. And I learned a lot more that way than if I had allowed myself to be part of a system,--an inmate of an institution. . . . All strive for the same goal--all worship the same stupid god--the god of bigness and sameness. Be yourself and don't be part of a gang...!

Travel Number

Judge

PRICE, 10 CENTS
JUNE 10, 1911

Judge An American Queen

June 17, 1911

While studying in England, Flagg saw the works of John Singer Sargent and decided that he wanted to be a portrait painter. Even though Sargent was a great influence on his work, Flagg soon realized that he wanted more choice in subject matter and returned to illustration. It did not help that Flagg found Sargent, an American, to be more English than the English.

JAMES MONTGOMERY FLAGG

Leslie's Can This Be Done?

August 21, 1913

In the early 1900s, top illustrators were the movie stars of their day, each with his own "Girl." Charles Dana Gibson, of "Gibson Girl" fame, had plays and songs written about his famous creation, and women everywhere tried their hardest to emulate her impossibly elegant figure and bearing. Harrison Fisher and Howard Chandler Christy also had their own "Girls," and

AUGUST 21, 1913 PRICE 10 CENTS

Leslie's

ESTABLISHED IN 1855

Leslie's **Trouble in Mexico!**
October 23, 1913

images of their lovelies adorned the walls of homes of men and women alike in this country and abroad. The public eagerly awaited the next issue of the many illustrated weekly and monthly magazines, hoping for a new illustration by their favorite artist.

After Flagg returned to the United States in the beginning years of this century, he developed his own example

Leslie's
ESTA SHED IN 1855

of the fairer sex. From the beginning, Flagg's "Girl" was a natural beauty, a really good-looking girl-next-door. She was sexier than her illustrated sisters, and Flagg drew her in such a way that one senses that she was well aware of the facts of life. In fact, Flagg was considered to be an expert in female pulchritude and was often invited to judge beauty pageants. By 1932, he had come to

The September 15 Cents
American
Magazine
JAMES
MONTGOMERY
FLAGG'S
I Should Say So
Every Month

Boston Sunday Post
February 7, 1915

dread being approached, and was quoted in The New York *Times* commenting on an university's invitation: "Sure--I'll pick out the prettiest gals--if any--or if six. All sorts of colleges every year do this to me...and I have had to gaze on some of the most god-awful female mugs in this broad tho' narrow land!"

In three covers we can see the unabashed nature of Flagg's creation.

Boston Sunday Post

SUNDAY MAGAZINE

PART 5
20 PAGES

BOSTON, MASS.
FEBRUARY 7, 1915

DO YOU
KNOW A
MORROW
MAN
?

JAMES MONTGOMERY FLAGG

The Red Cross Magazine
October 1917

The beautiful and ambitious woman in *Prize For Best Title* (*Judge,* November 1, 1924) searches the "Aristocratic Yellow Pages" for the right nobleman to marry while her Latin sister causes *Trouble in Mexico* (*Leslie's,* October 23, 1913), for our troops there. In a third illustration, she forgets her traditional role by proposing on bended knee, which leaves us with the unusual question, "Will He or Won't He?" (*Life,* April 16, 1908).

October 1917 THE Twenty Cents

RED CROSS

MAGAZINE

Still, Flagg's "Men" were not pushovers, as the artist displayed in his World War I posters. When the war started in Europe in 1914, most Americans were united in their desire to remain neutral. To them, Europe represented out-of-date monarchies and ancient feuds. While Woodrow Wilson stated that America would stay out of the war, a number of people--Teddy Roosevelt being the most prominent--

JAN 19th 1918
Leslie's
Illustrated Weekly
PRICE 10 CENTS
In Canada 15 Cents
Notice to Reader
When you finish reading this magazine place a one cent stamp alongside of this notice, hand same to any postal employe and it will be placed in the hands of our soldiers or sailors at the front.
A. S. BURLESON,
AMERICA'S BIT
JAMES MONTGOMERY FLAGG

believed that America should prepare just in case. A number of artists, including Flagg, felt strongly about America's unpreparedness, and as early as 1916 he designed a poster for the Naval Consulting Board's Committee on Industrial Preparedness, showing the Venus de Milo wrapped in the American flag with the caption "Armless."

By early 1917, it looked like America must enter the fight. While working

Judge

August 16, 1919
Price 10 Cents

Judge Prize For Best Title
November 1, 1924

with a New York preparedness committee, Flagg made the first three-sheet lithographic poster of the war, *Wake Up, America!*, showing Columbia asleep with storm clouds gathered ominously in the background. Flagg's "Girls" were now drafted for the duration, and they came to personify not only the United States, but also France and Britain (*All For One And One For All!!/Vive La France!*; *Side By Side - Britannia!*). Her sex appeal was

JUDGE
NOVEMBER 1, 1924 ★
PRICE 15 CENTS
BURKE'S PEERAGE
"PRIZE FOR BEST TITLE"
JAMES MONTGOMERY FLAGG

not gone, only toned down--most likely to keep the public's attention on the war effort. Simultaneously, his "Men" slipped quickly into uniform to encourage Americans to enlist in the Army, Navy, and Marine Corps.

When the United States entered the war in April 1917, Flagg worked with the government's Division of

JAMES MONTGOMERY FLAGG

Pictorial Publicity (headed by Charles Dana Gibson), which coordinated propaganda efforts by artists and illustrators. Literally thousands of art works were submitted to Gibson's committee with subject matter ranging from recruitment to war relief. Flagg was very prolific in his poster submissions, but his most famous poster, *I Want You For U.S. Army,* with the stern and pointing Uncle Sam, had been done as a

WAKE UP
AMERICA
DAY
APRIL 19
1917

magazine cover for *Leslie's* in July 1916. The government printed 350,000 copies for recruitment and over one million for other patriotic purposes. In Flagg's *Uncle Sam,* gone was the folksy conception by previous artists, replaced by a muscular man who meant business.

Flagg also changed the public's perception of the Marine Corps. The phrase "Tell that to the Marines" had

I WANT YOU
FOR U.S. ARMY
NEAREST RECRUITING STATION

meant that the Marines were so gullible, you could tell them anything and they would believe it. In his poster, the artist showed a man taking off his coat for a fight, having read of some German war atrocity. The phrase now meant that if you told the Marines of an outrage, they would do something about it.

After the war, Flagg worked on one- and two-reel films, mainly comedies,

STAGE WOMEN'S
WAR RELIEF

with such names as *Independence B'gosh* and *Perfectly Fiendish Flanagan*. In the latter film, for example, Flagg poked fun at William S. Hart, the silent movie cowboy star whose films were sometimes very predictable. These films were produced on the East Coast, but Flagg also made many subsequent visits to Hollywood where, in addition to movie making, he sketched such stars as Gary Cooper and Marlene Dietrich.

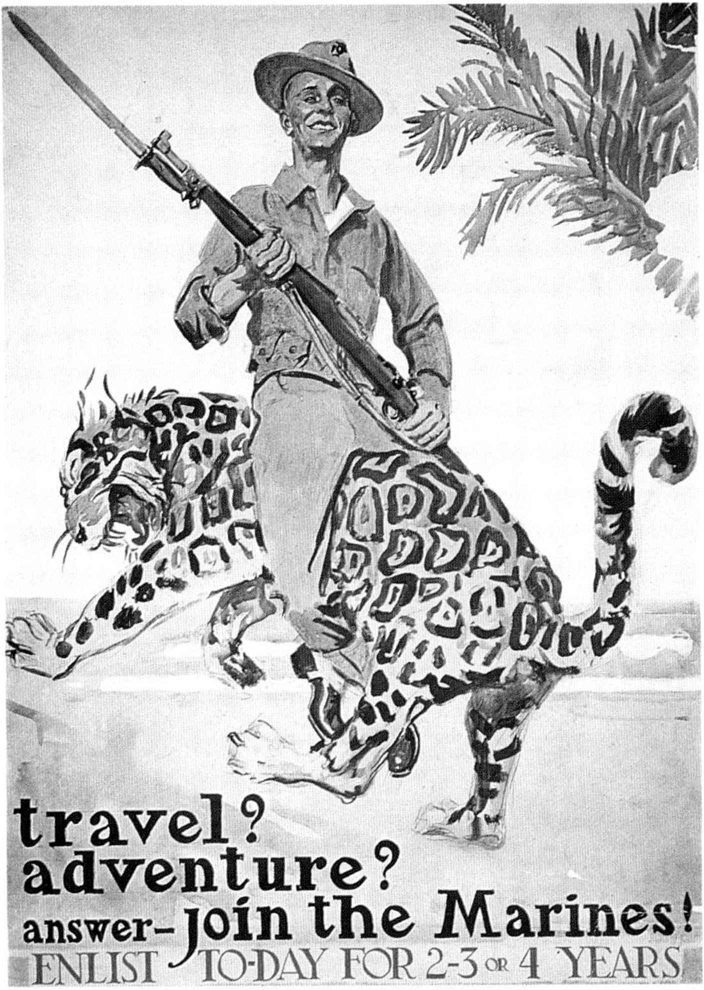
travel?
adventure?
answer– join the Marines!
ENLIST TO-DAY FOR 2-3 OR 4 YEARS

Our Regular Divisions Poster
1918

In 1924, Flagg married one of his models, Dorothy Fitch, by whom he had his only child, Faith. In his autobiography, he rarely talked of this second marriage, but he does give more attention to his first. In 1899, when Flagg was twenty-two and just out of the Art Students' League, he met Nellie McCormick, a socialite from St. Louis

OUR
REGULAR DIVISIONS
JAMES MONTGOMERY FLAGG
Honored and Respected by All
Enlist for the Infantry–
or in one of the other 12 branches.
Nearest Recruiting Office:

who was eleven years his senior. Both of their families were unhappy about their relationship, but the two persevered and were married. Unfortunately for Flagg, Nellie was more of a distant "Gibson Girl" type than the red-blooded "Flagg Girl," and the marriage became strained. It ended with Nellie's death in 1923.

ALL FOR ONE AND ONE FOR ALL!
VIVE LA FRANCE!
JAMES MONTGOMERY FLAGG

Side By Side-Britannia! Poster
1918

When not at work in his studio, Flagg had a very active social life. He was one of the founding members of the Dutch Treat Club in New York, where he wrote and acted in many of the annual shows. Before one show, John Barrymore, the famous actor, helped Flagg with his makeup for his part as the Devil, and was so taken by how Flagg looked, he told Flagg that he really

SIDE BY SIDE—
BRITANNIA!

should have been an actor. Flagg thought that this was an interesting remark since Barrymore had always wanted to be an artist. Unfortunately, John Barrymore was no artist, and Flagg later wrote that Barrymore, "couldn't draw for nuts!" The two were life-long friends, and Flagg considered him, "a great scholar, a great actor, a

TELL THAT TO THE MARINES!
AT 24 EAST 23rd STREET
HUNS KILL WOMEN AND CHILDREN!
JAMES MONTGOMERY FLAGG

First In The Fight Poster
ca. 1918

great conversationalist, a great companion, and a great wit," attributes which could be applied to Flagg as well.

As he grew older, the changes in the "fine arts" baffled Flagg. He could not understand the appeal of modern art and he hated Picasso and all the Impressionists, except for Monet whom he thought a great landscape painter.

FIRST IN THE FIGHT-
ALWAYS FAITHFUL-
BE A U.S. MARINE!

Together We Win Poster

ca. 1918

For Flagg, the artistic process was straight-forward:

> First, you have a hell of a lot of talent . . . then you have a lot of experience; then you have a lot of knowledge; then you have a lot of taste; then you have understanding, intuition, imagination, craftsmanship, red blood, philosophy, a fine canvas, the best paints, and some one or something

U.S.NAVY
JAMES MONTGOMERY FLAGG
TOGETHER WE WIN

that demands your entire concentration. The result is a fine canvas.(from *Roses and Buckshot*, his autobiography)

When Flagg died on May 27, 1960, he was survived by his second wife and daughter. In his will, as reported in The New York *Times* (June 4, 1960), he wrote, "I leave my warm love to my friends, as I'm sure they know . . . that

Help him to help U.S.!
Help the Horse to Save the Soldier
JAMES MONTGOMERY FLAGG
THE AMERICAN RED STAR ANIMAL RELIEF

Hold Onto Uncle Sam's Insurance Poster
ca. 1919

life goes on--like it or lump it. . ." Life has gone on, but Flagg's death closed a chapter on the career of one of America's greatest and most interesting illustrators.

HOLD ON TO UNCLE SAM'S INSURANCE

Vignettes

Vignettes